I0486105

Counting the Letter

Kid's Coloring book

By

S.B. Nozaz

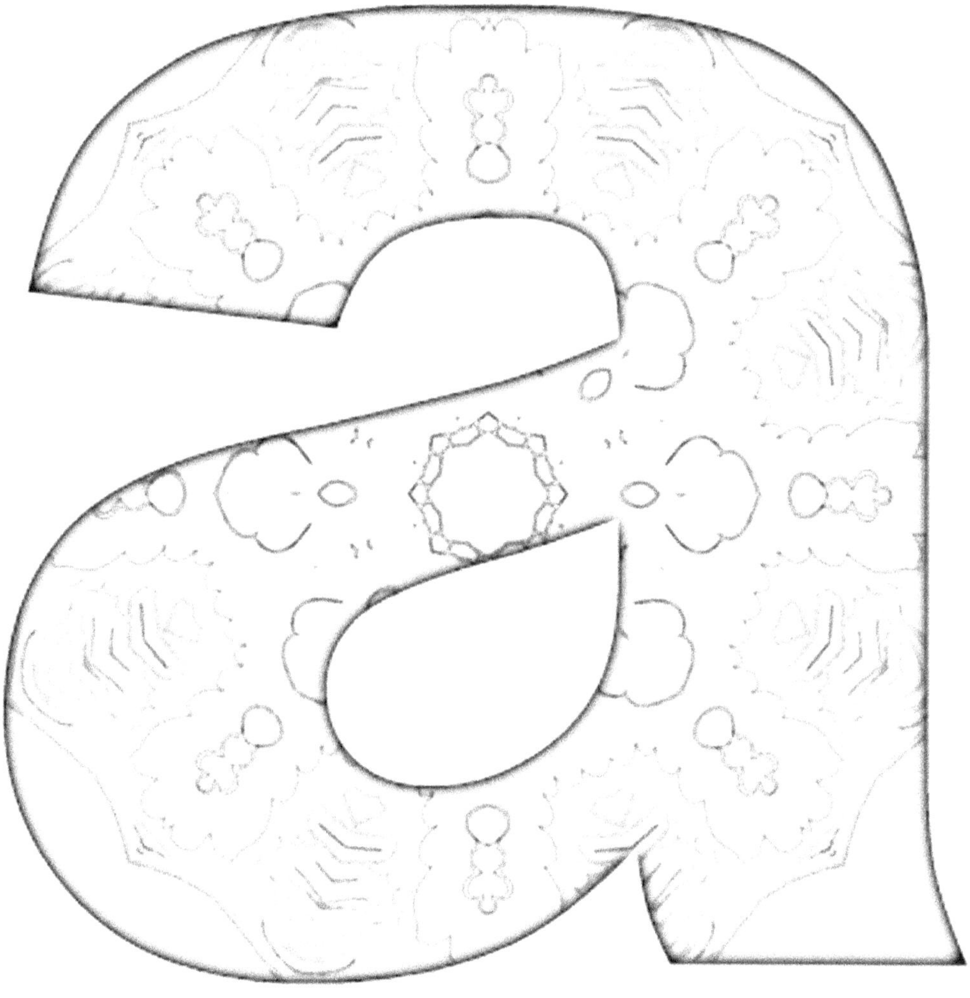

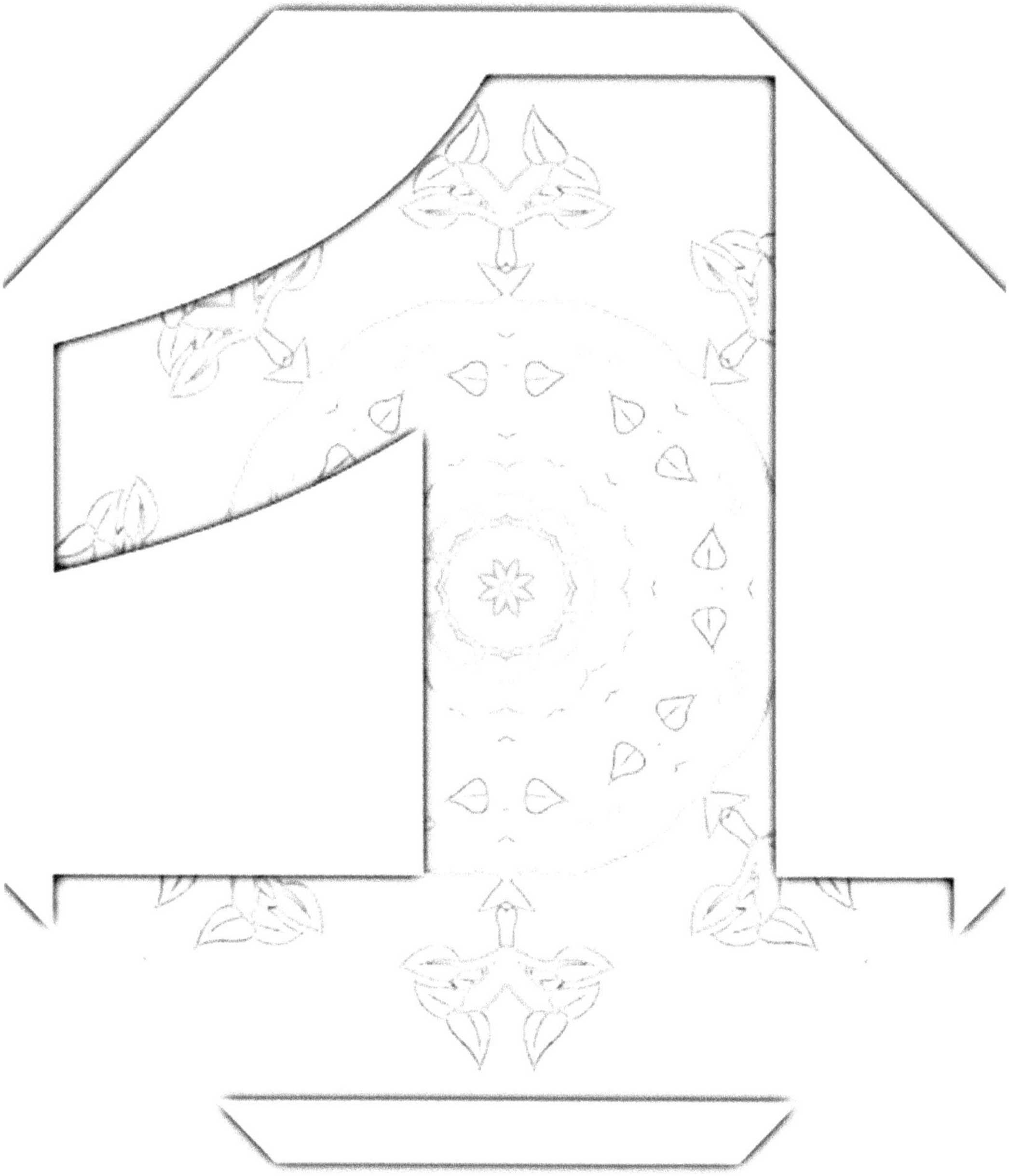

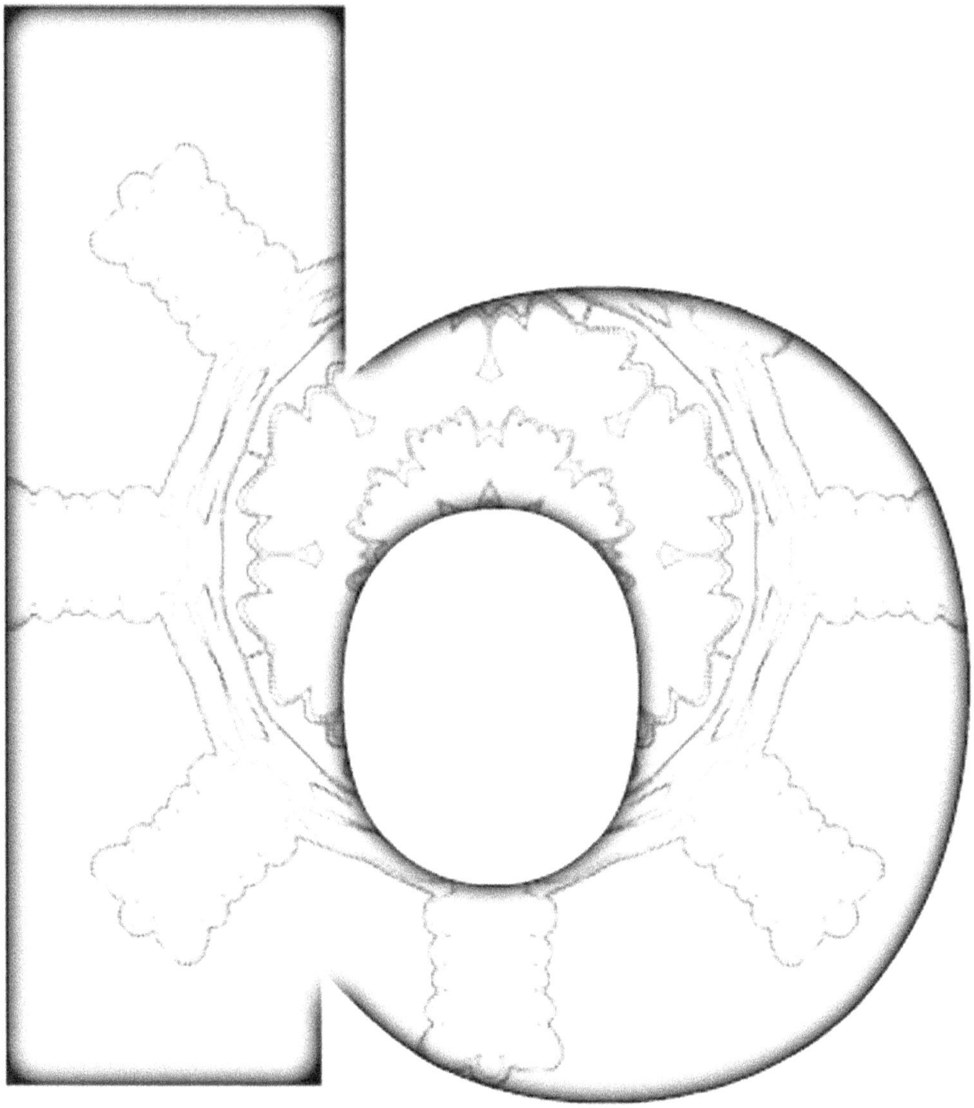
b

2

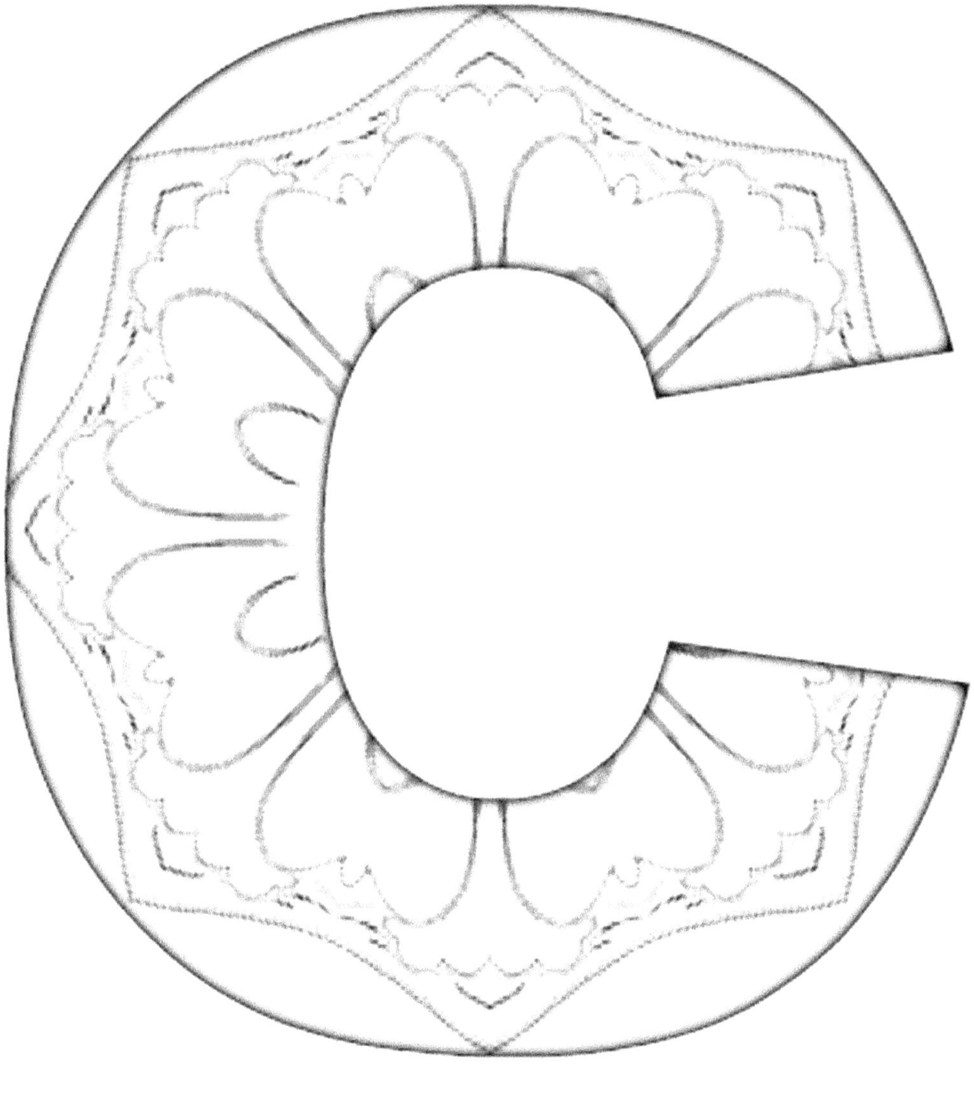

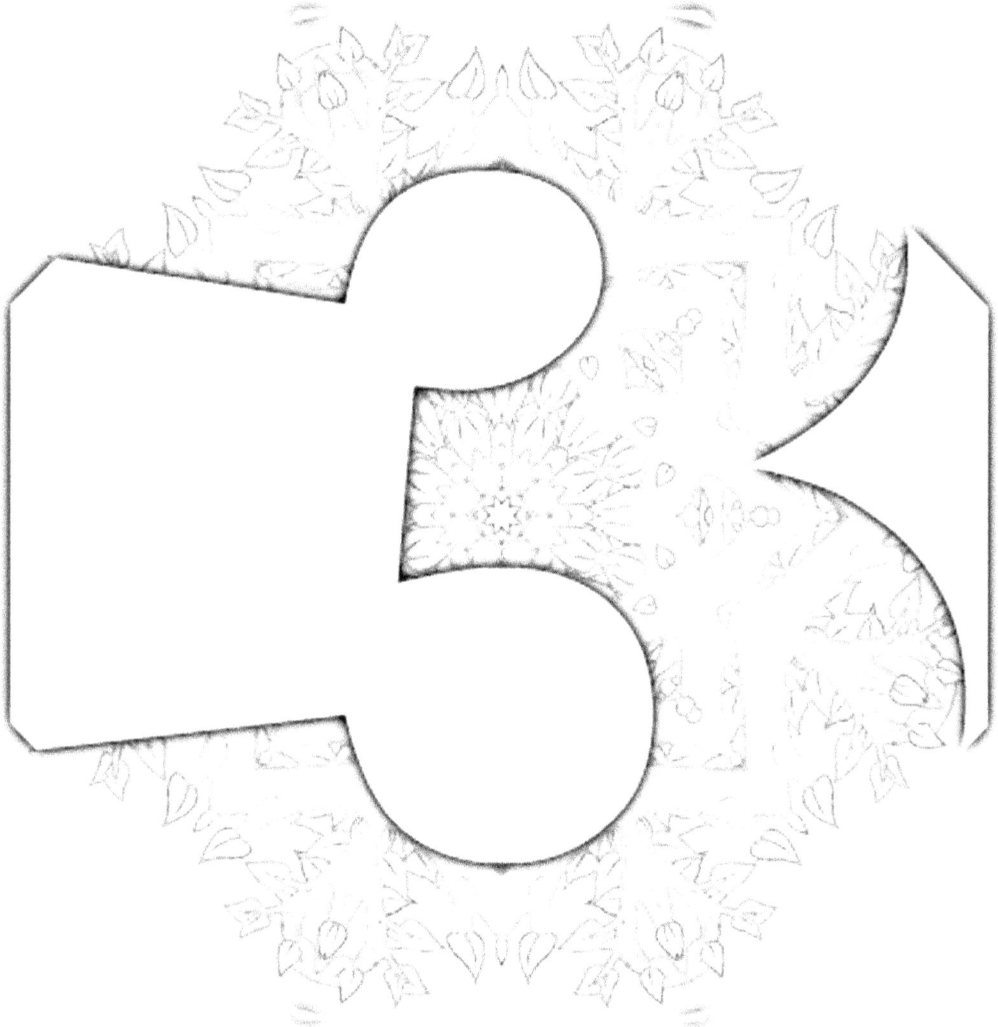
13

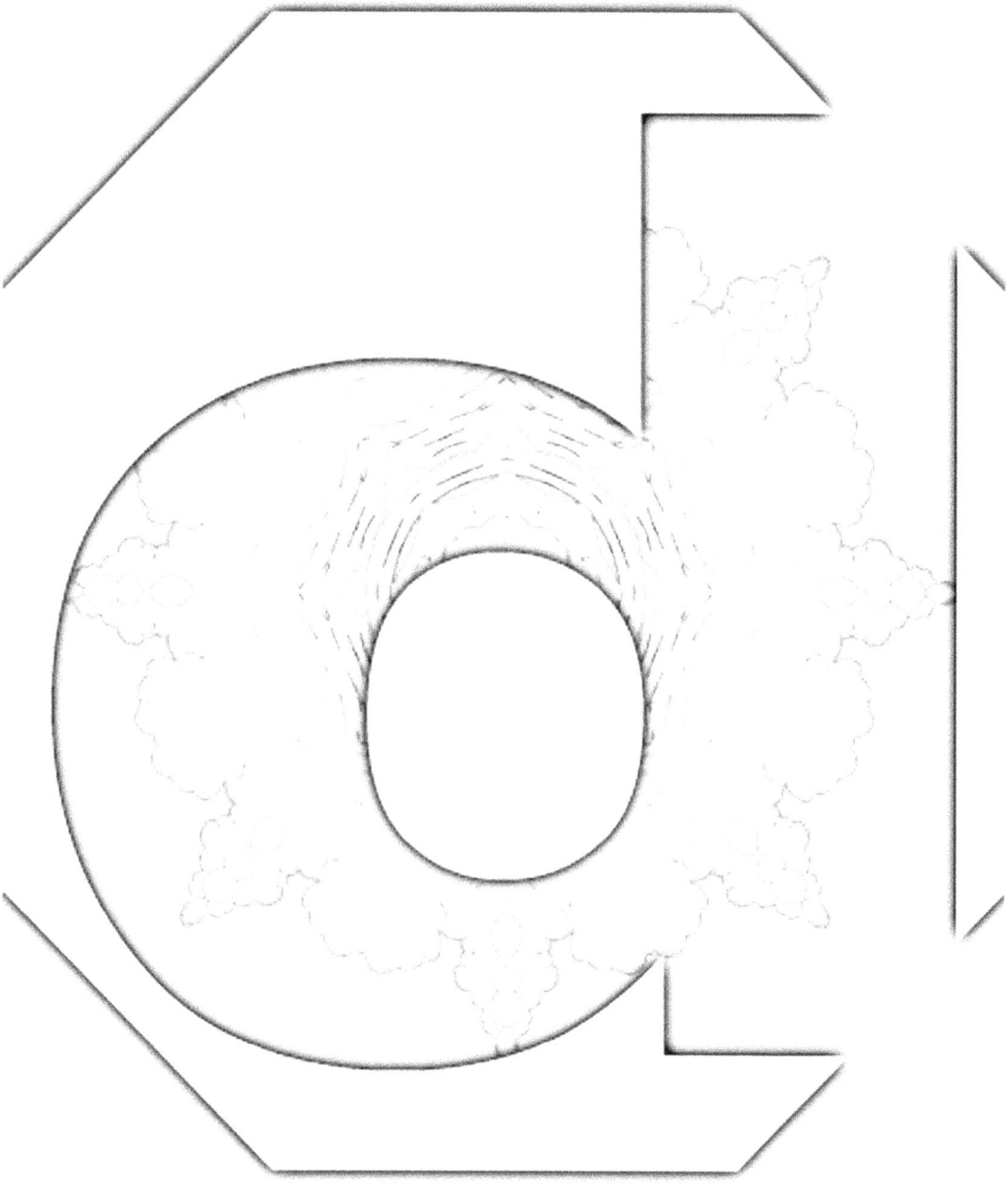

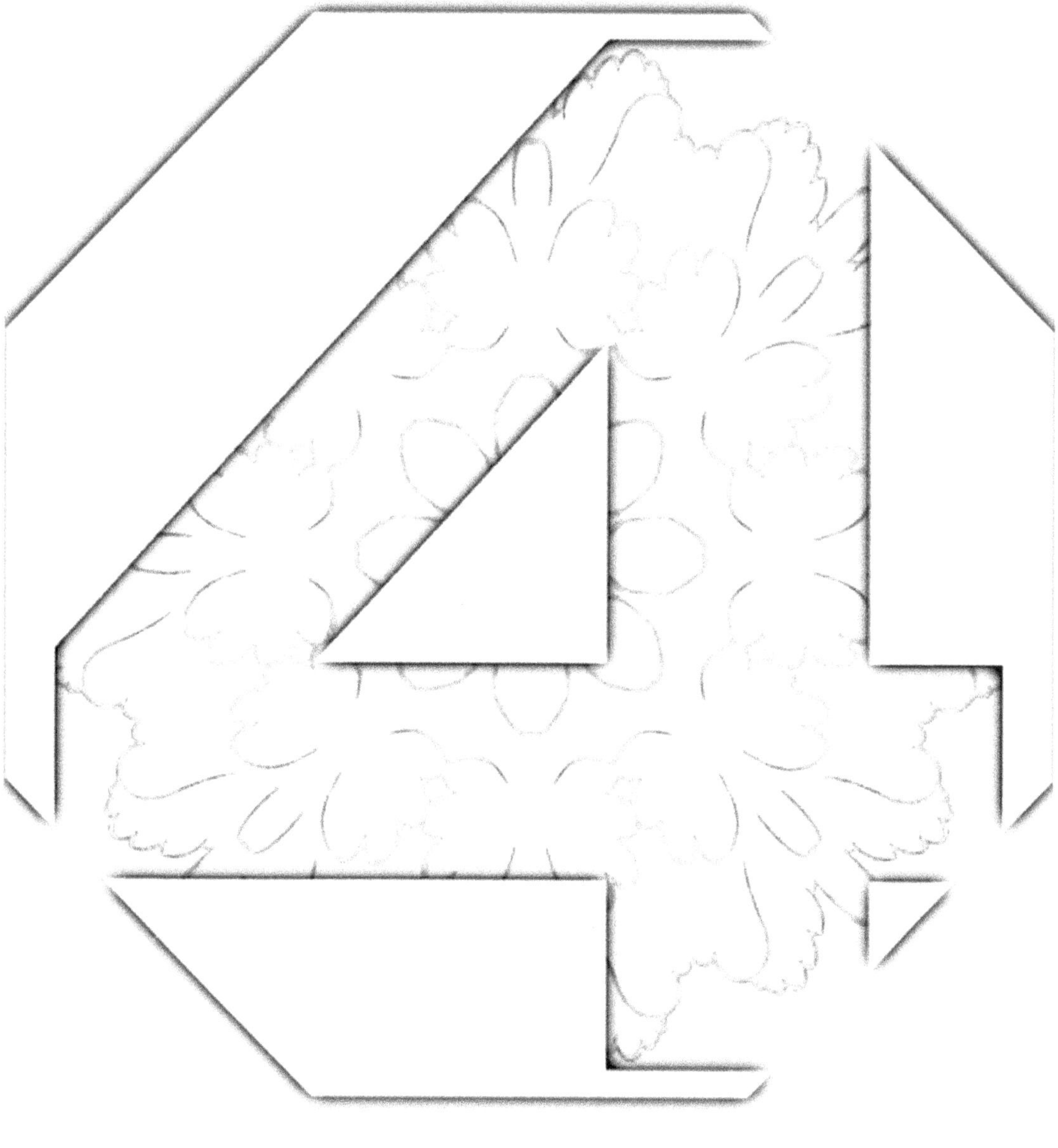

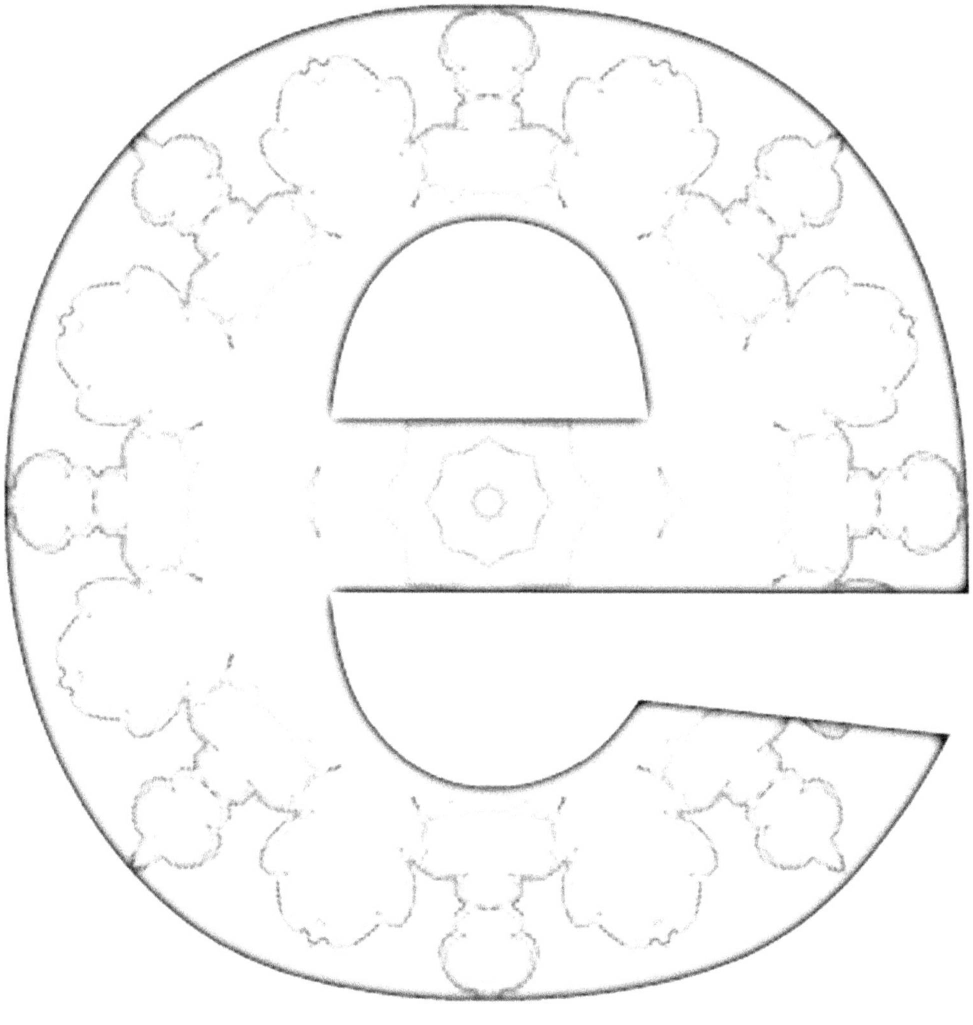
e

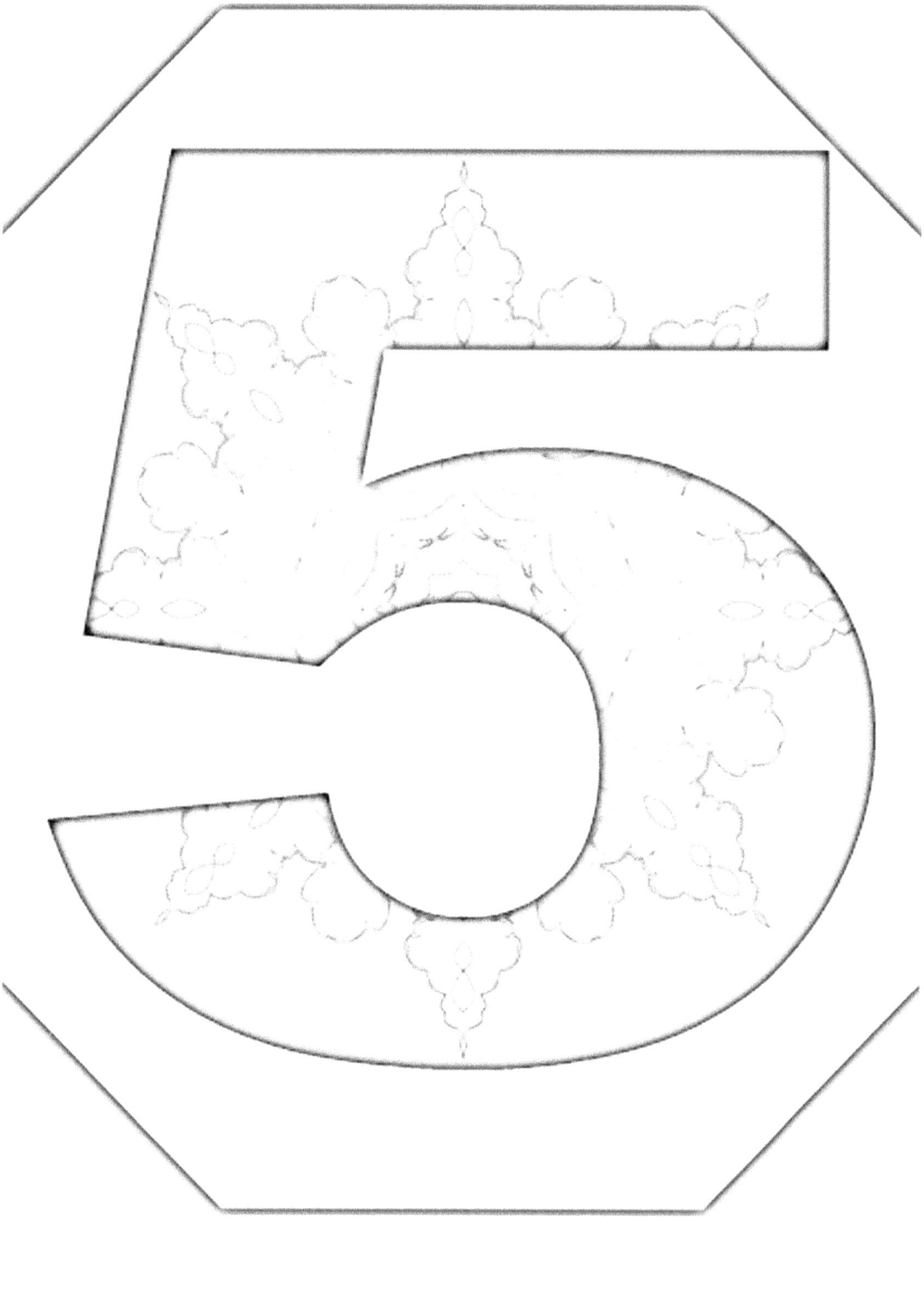
5

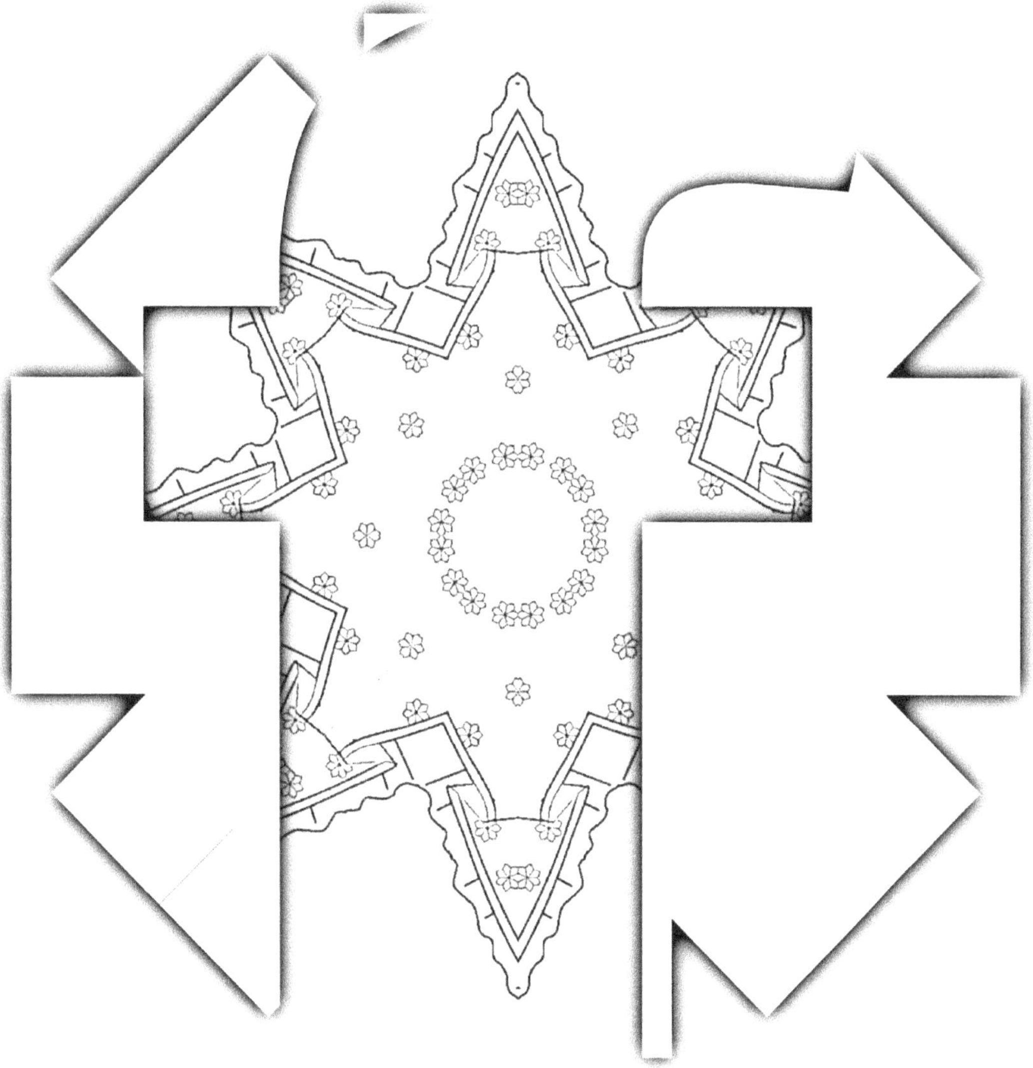

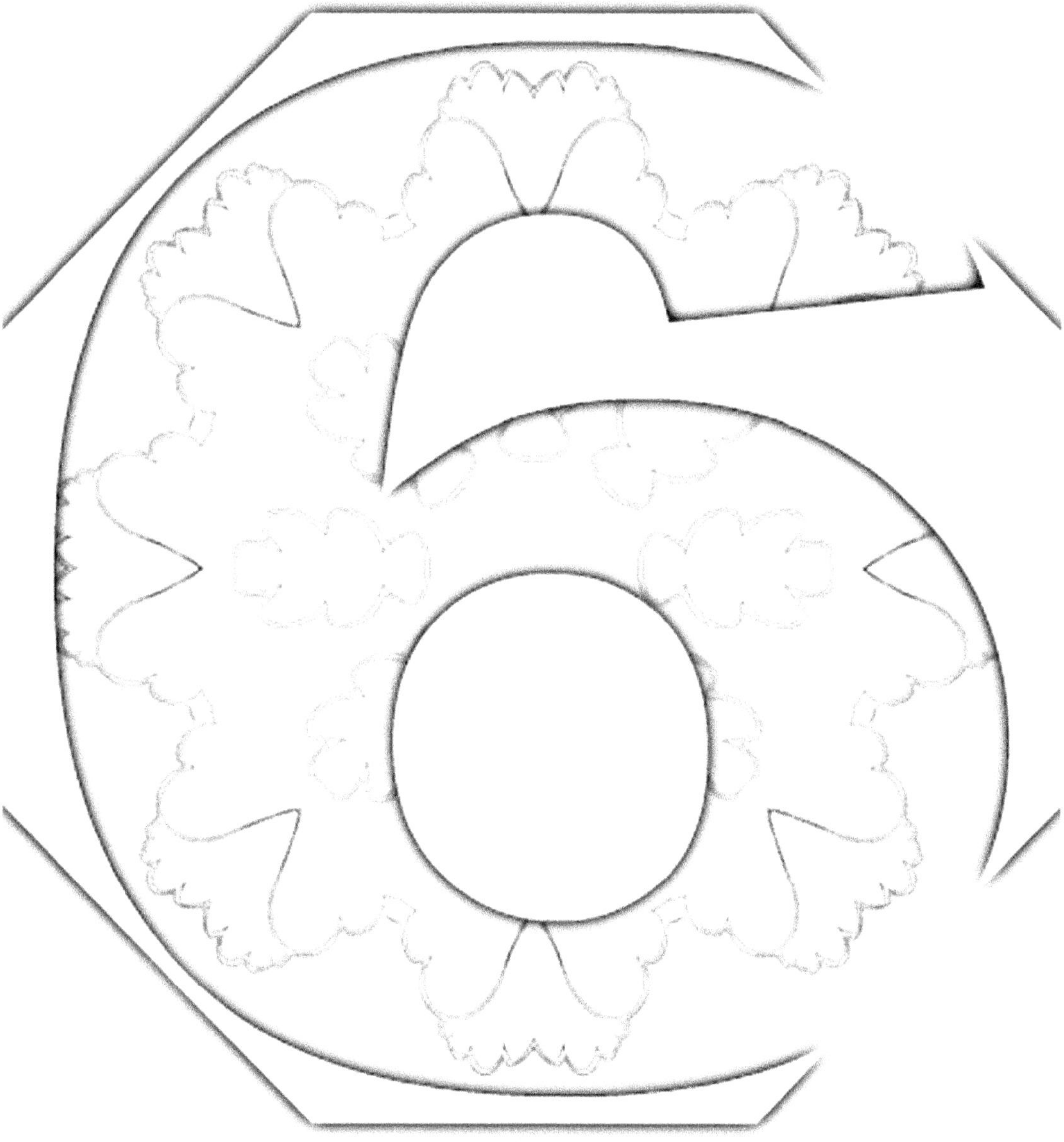

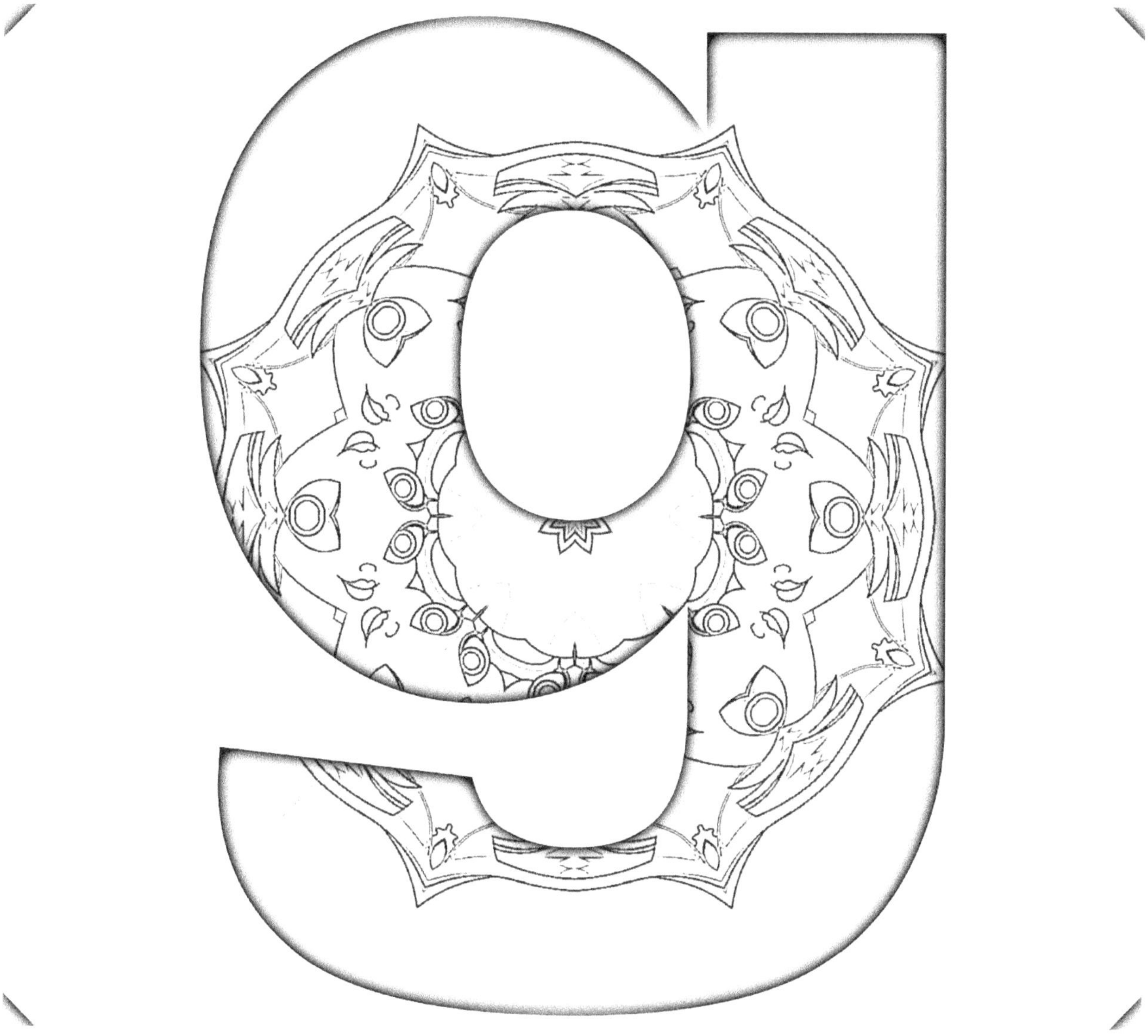

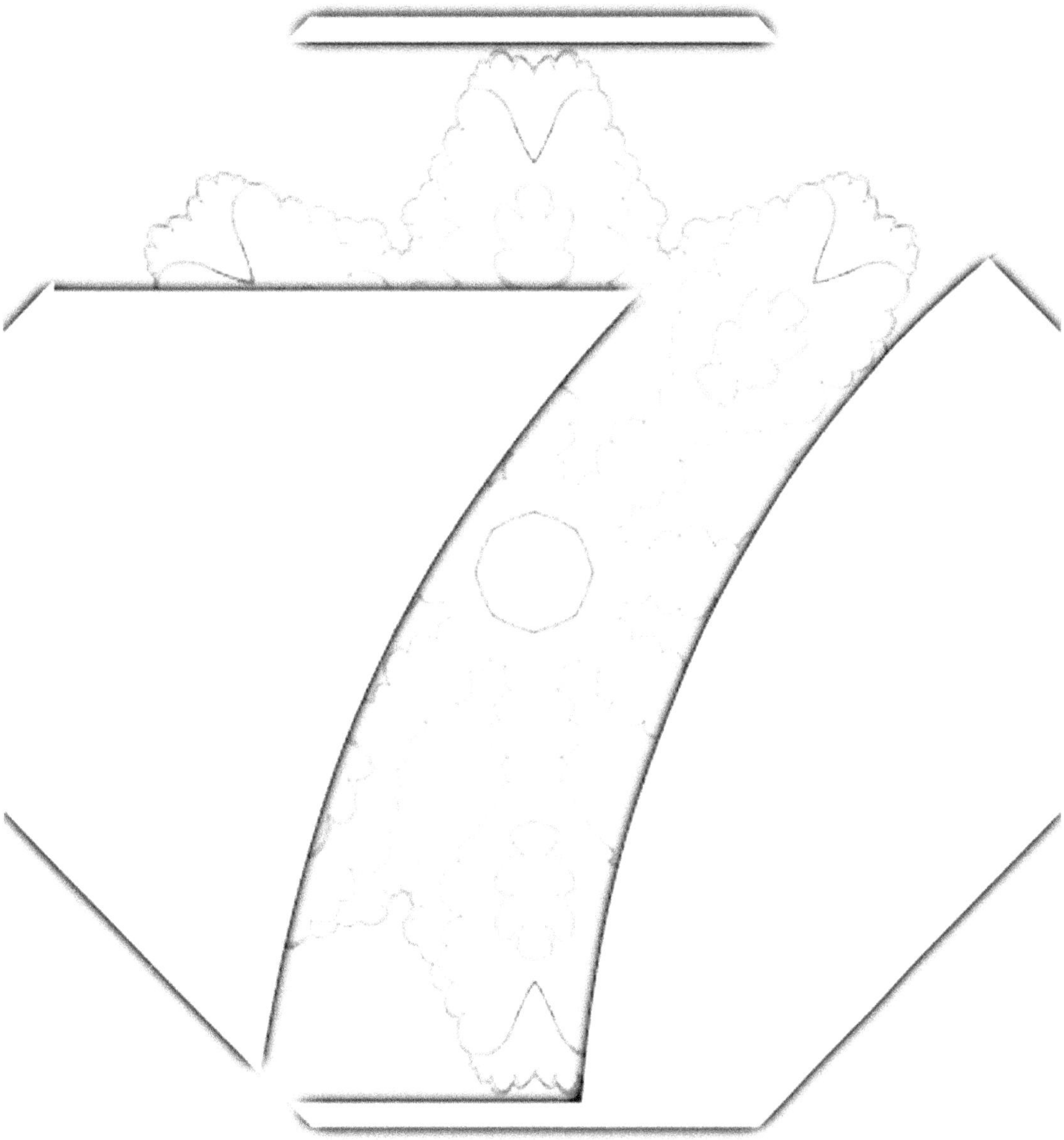
7

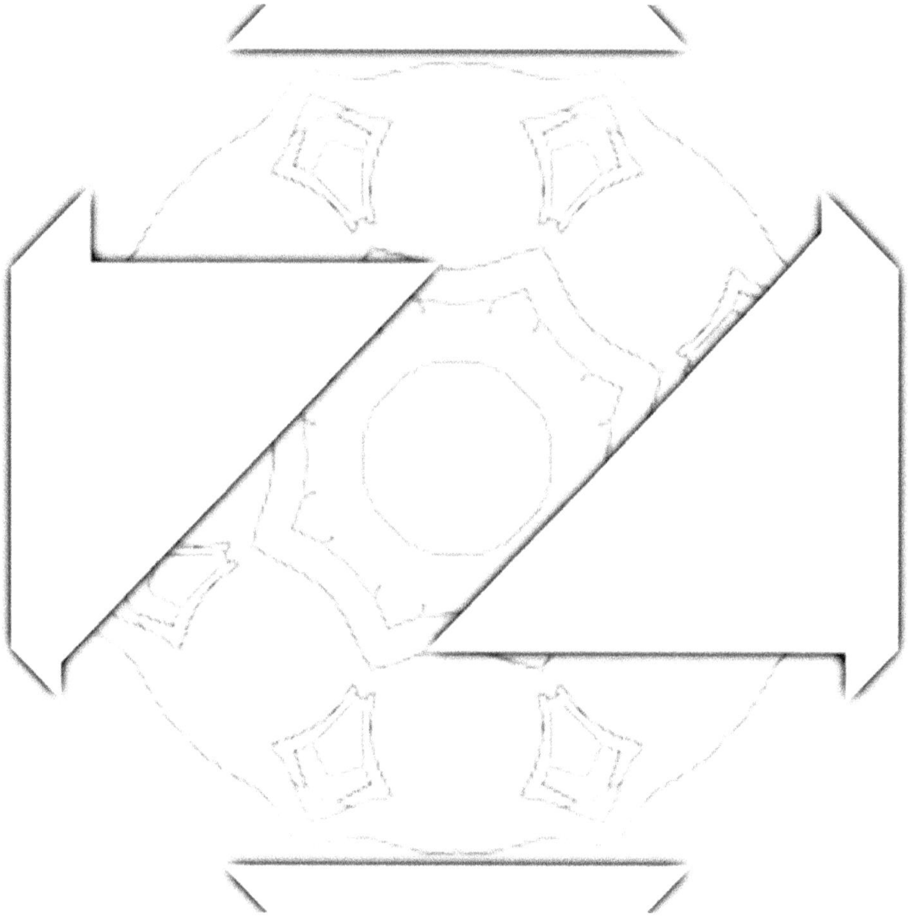

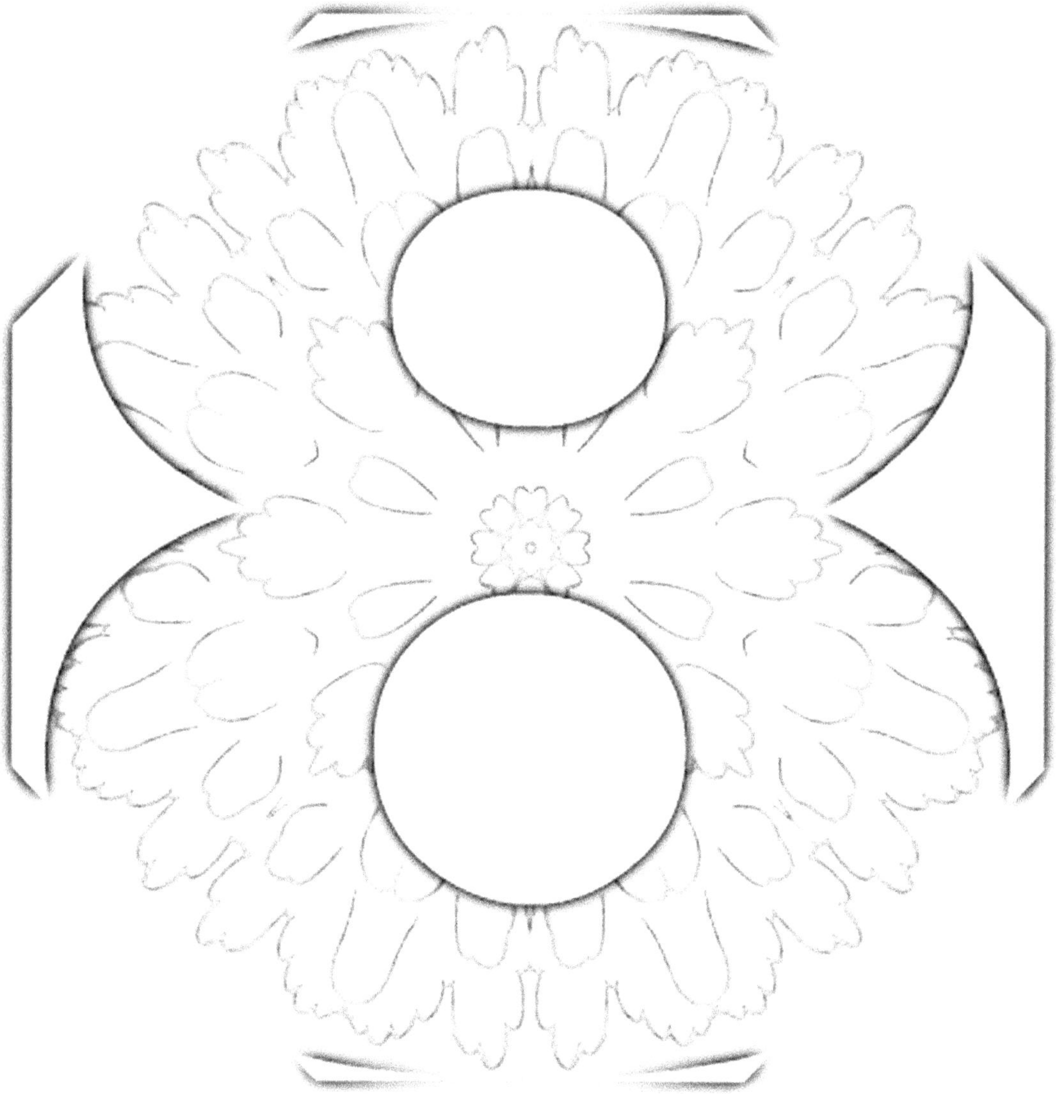

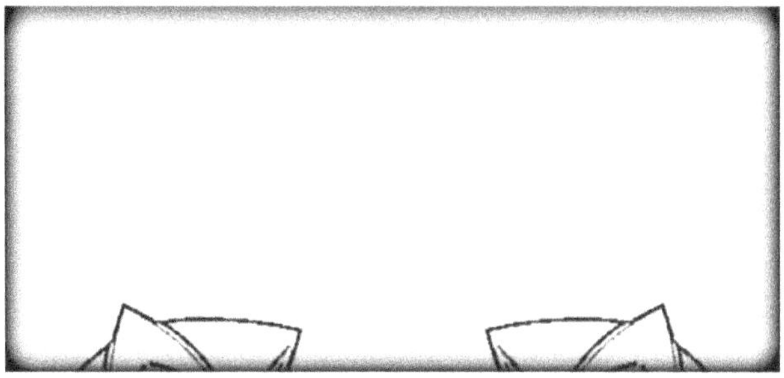

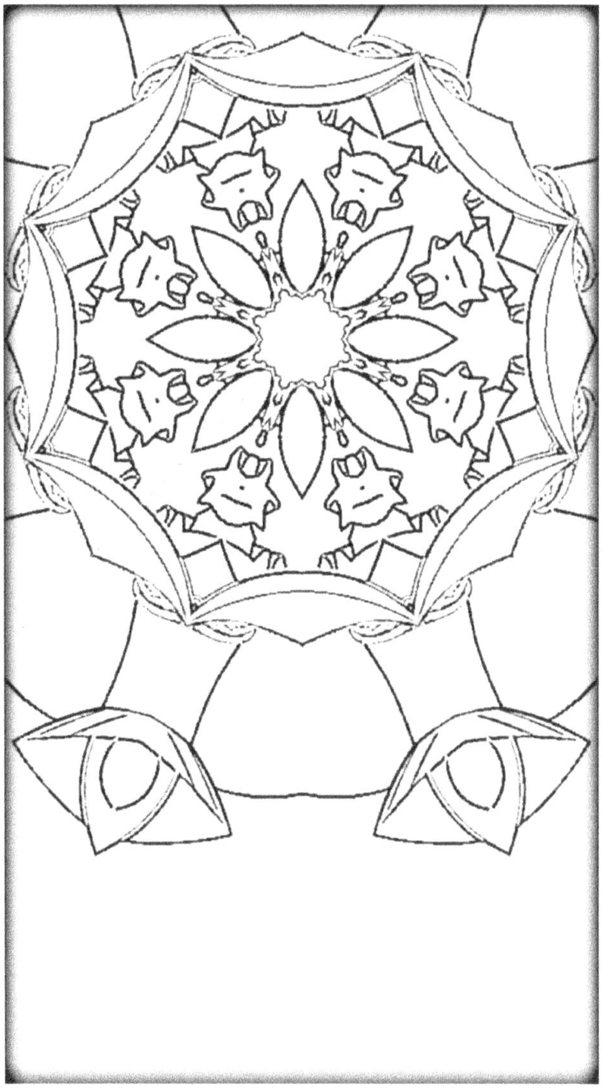

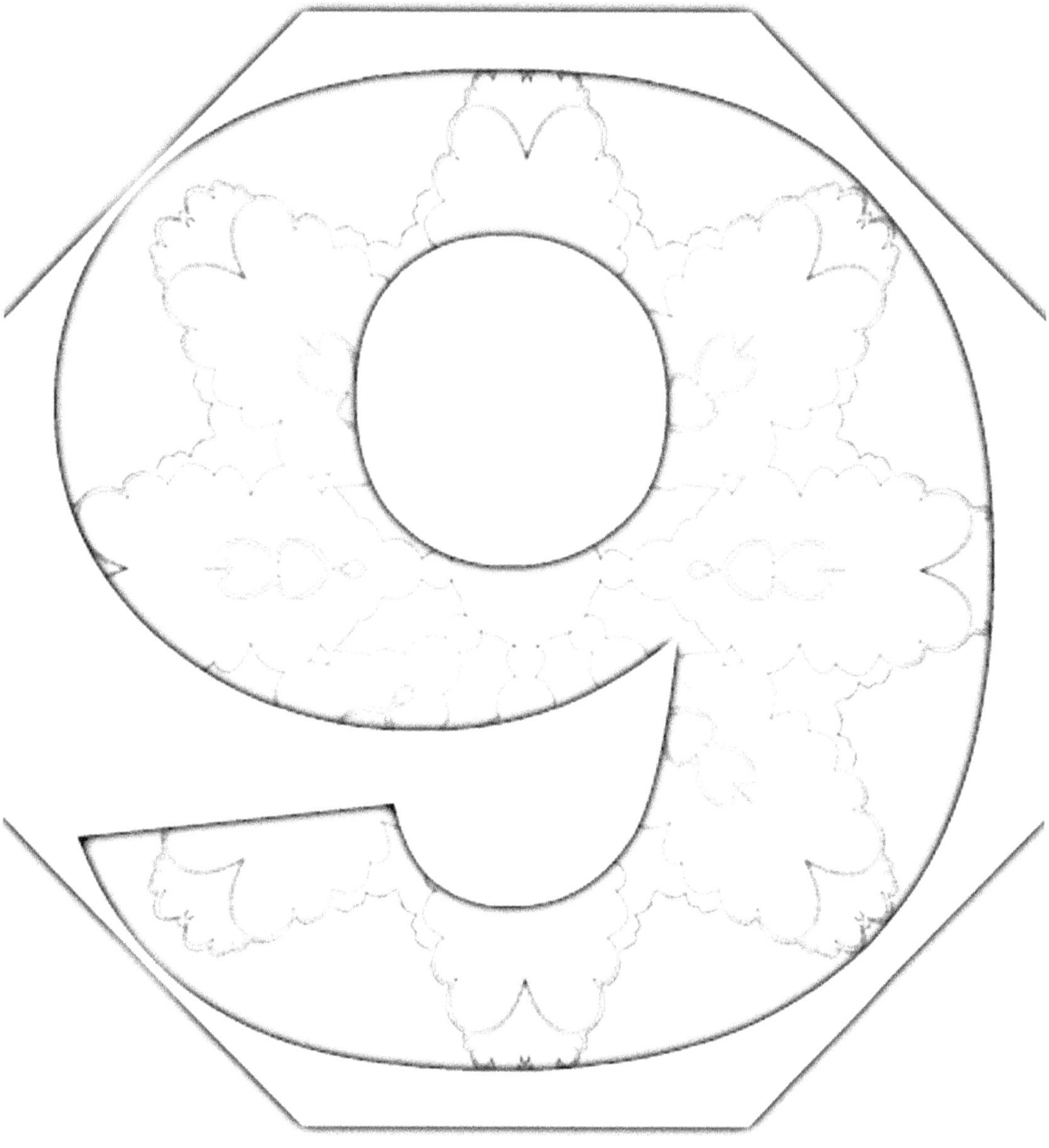
9

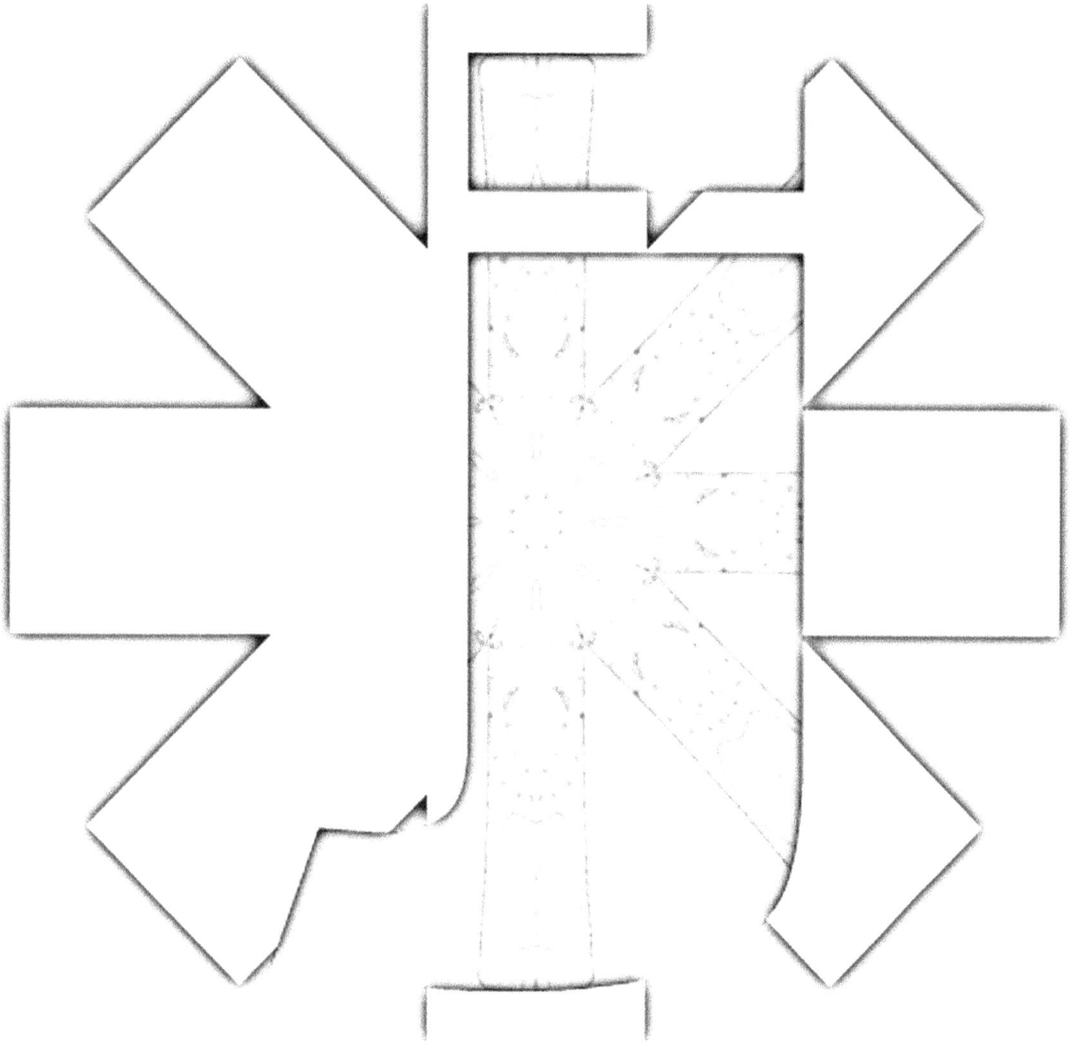

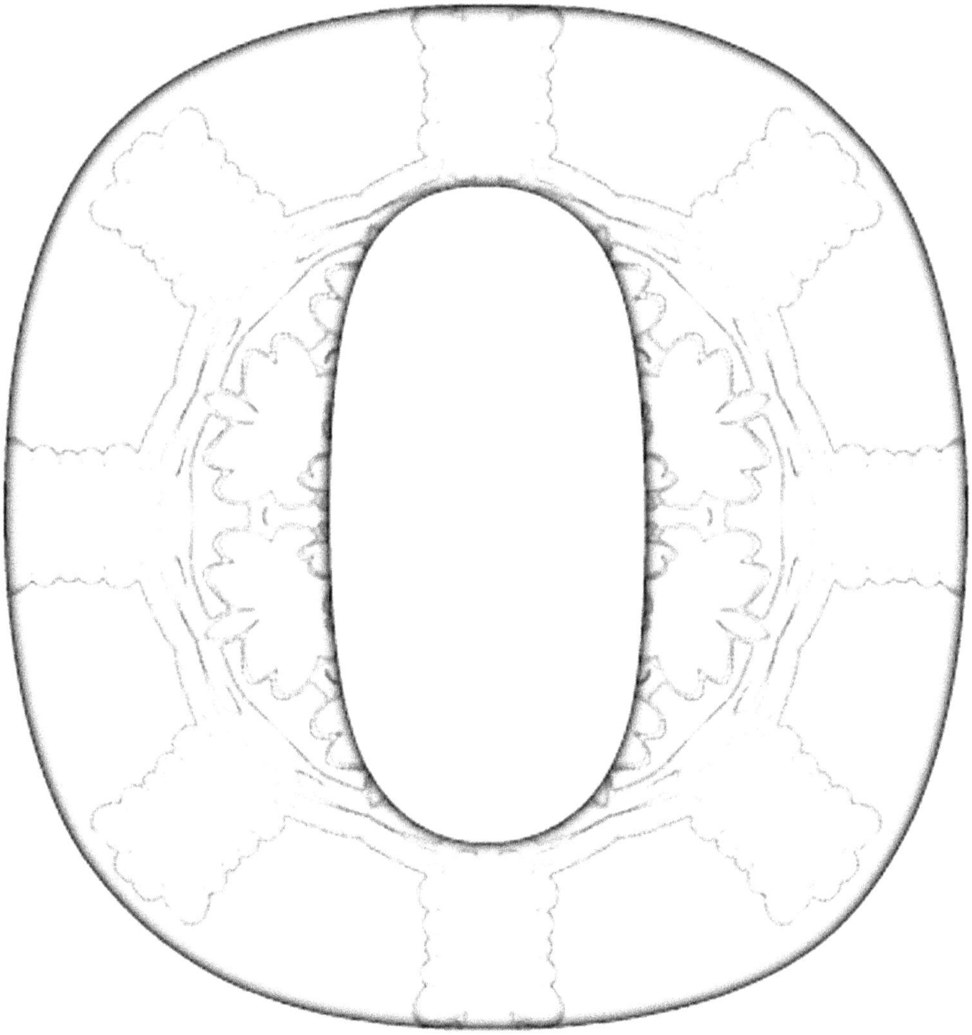

Note

www.ingramcontent.com/pod-product-compliance
Lightning Source LLC
Chambersburg PA
CBHW080651180526
45168CB00008B/3388
9781517472504